DASHED DREAMS AND DIAMONDS

Dangerous Memories and Impatient Truths

Stories

From

Seven Women

of the

Gospel

Patricia Clemens Repikoff

WIPF & STOCK · Eugene, Oregon

Wipf and Stock Publishers
199 W 8th Ave, Suite 3
Eugene, OR 97401

Dashed Dreams and Diamonds
Stories From Seven Women of the Gospels
By Repikoff, Patricia Clemens
Copyright©1998 by Repikoff, Patricia Clemens
ISBN 13: 978-1-55635-983-5
Publication date 9/1/2008
Previously published by Friends from St. Therese Parish, Seattle, 1998

"Blessed is she who trusts that the promises made to her by God will be fulfilled." —Luke 1: 45

For girls and young women everywhere...

Let your longing,
your restlessness

for the
MORE

in life
be sung strong and true,
unsilenced!

One day all our song will
split this closed world
WIDE OPEN!

—Feast of Perpetua and Felicity,
Early Christian Martyrs

This poetic envisioning of seven biblical wo/men whose stories are told in the gospels, is an important contribution to a hermeneutics of imagination. Patty Repikoff challenges her readers to imagine these wo/men differently. For, not only rational logic but also imaginative participation is at work whenever we read or hear biblical texts. Yet, our biblical imagination has been deformed not only by religious dogmatism and historical positivism but also by linguistic androcentrism since grammatically masculine so-called generic language marginalizes wo/men and makes them invisible. By re-imagining these seven wo/men in a poetic and dramatic fashion *Dashed Dreams and Diamonds* enables readers to engage with them both creatively and critically.

If feminist theologians seek to place wo/men's struggles for survival and transformation in the center of their critical re-visioning of Scripture and traditions, feminist poets seek to fashion both a "new optic" and a "different voice" that can see the world anew and break through androcentric marginalization and silence. In antiquity the poets were called "theologians" because they were considered to be inspired. As in antiquity so also today feminist poets are the seers and prophets of their people, who are wo/men, proclaiming new visions and self-understandings. They enable us to envision the past, present, and future of wo/men differently, they create "dangerous memories and impatient truth." For as Toni Morrison so forcefully states in her novel *Beloved:*

> She did not tell them to clean up their lives or to go and sin no more. She did not tell them they were the blessed of the earth, its inheriting meek or its glory bound pure. She told them that the only grace they could have, was the grace they could imagine. That if they could not see it, they would not have it. [p.88]

I am grateful to Patricia Repikoff that through her poetry and her truly prophetic ministry she has opened up new visions of grace for all of us!

Elisabeth Schüssler Fiorenza
Harvard University
April 1998

TABLE OF CONTENTS

INTRODUCTION

> "What would happen if one
> Woman told the truth
> of her life?
> The world would split open!"
>
> Muriel Rukeyser
> "Käthe Kollwitz"

The poem-stories you are about to read represent my attempt to enter the world of silence shared by the women who inhabit the Gospel stories. With study and prayer, I listened carefully and imaginatively to, under, around, into, and behind the few descriptions afforded these women in the actual Gospel stories. Gradually their voices and memories of sorrow and liberation emerged full and strong. Their stories seemed to split open the thick curtain of silence which had surrounded them and kept them locked away, apart from me, and from all of us, for far too long. As I finished writing these stories I realized that they indeed had split my own world wide open; these women had befriended me. I had received seven Gospel sisters who knew how to share my journey, who were willing to walk with me on the long road of fear and faith, anger and joy, death and resurrection.

Several years ago I had the opportunity to study the Gospels in greater depth, and enthusiastically read the work of many fine scripture scholars. Among them, Elisabeth Schüssler Fiorenza caught my attention. She taught me how to read between the lines, how to ask questions about what was missing from the scriptures, how to be suspicious about the silences.

Even before I began studying, I had been aware that the Gospels recounted many occasions when Jesus broke through the law and customs of his day to teach, embrace, and heal women. I was aware how Jesus affirmed and offered new possibilities to women in an age of unquestioned patriarchy. However, as I reflected on the Gospel stories which told of Jesus' encounters with women, I found little elaboration on each woman's experience of Jesus as a healer and liberator. And so, I began to ask questions: "What would happen if the women whose lives were deeply affected by Jesus could tell of their experience with Him?" . . . "What would happen if Mary of Nazareth, or the 'Bent Over Woman' could share her memories with us?"

Those questions served as the beginning of this endeavor. I chose seven Gospel women who had always intrigued me. I researched, piecing together as much background information as I could find about each of them, taking careful notes. Then, I put the notes aside and began to meditate, using my active imagination. For many nights these women entered my imagination and heart. They developed faces: some of them took on the appearance of the poor and suffering in our cities, those who wait in food lines and who sleep in shelters; others reminded me of the Mothers of the Disappeared who stand in South American plazas, demanding justice and freedom for their people; still others seemed similar to my friends who daily struggle for full equality and security for women in schools, work, and the church.

Their stories found voices in poetic form; their bodies started to move. I began to imagine these seven women telling their stories as did the Black women in Ntozake Shange's poignant choreopoem, *For Colored Girls Who Have Considered Suicide/When the Rainbow is Enuf.* I envisioned these seven women sharing their memories and truth in church sanctuaries, basements, and on stages before groups of women, men, and children.

Once the stories were recorded in poetic and dramatic form, friends began to read them, and identify with all or one of the women. Seven classmates dared to dance and tell these women's stories at a prayer service. Since the first public, prayerful storytelling of the *Dangerous Memories and Impatient Truths,* there have been many more. The poems have been shared at retreats, reconciliation and healing services; they have served as homilies as Eucharist; high school students have enacted them. After one performance, two six-year-old girls asked if they could read and practice the dancing at home so when they became old they too could tell the stories.

As you begin this book, I invite you to read the stories slowly, perhaps aloud, savoring the words, the mystery of these images and memories, allowing the truth of these lives to split (or even pry) open the memories and the truth of your own dashed dreams and diamonds.

Patricia Repikoff

Mary of Nazareth

A woman who grew up with the strong will, courage, and compassion which led her to receive God's Spirit and Word in a most
open and terrifying way. As Jesus' mother, she finds her faith in
God tested to the breaking point. She becomes sister, friend, and
bearer of hope to all who dare trust in the often terrifying Spirit
of God, especially those women throughout the world whose children and dreams are "cut down too young."

MARY OF NAZARETH

I am mystery,
    rebel,
    mother,
    refugee,
    a voice crying out compassion
        in the face of cruelty,
            human misery.

I am Mary of Nazareth.
I sing my reckless trust,
    my ache,
        confusion.
Mine are the dirges any mother sings
        whose child is cut
        down too young.
I sing
    of dashed dreams
    that turned to diamonds.

I was young and hopeful,
    the future danced in my eyes!

I always had a wild streak
    (some said
    I was a rebel),
My head uncovered,
    my hair flying,
        I ran
        through the streets
            with friends.
My voice carried
    loudest,
    they said.

I did not always
    heed the Law,
        or my parents,
        or anyone else.

I sometimes spoke
            out.
I asked the why of things.
I was silenced,
    but never
    for long,
    because
    a restlessness ran through me.

It seemed I wanted more from life
        than most.
The longing wouldn't go away.

They hoped that Joseph would
        tame my restless spirit
        with domestic dreams, a family future.

I accepted,
  but secretly,
        I tucked away
        my restlessness
        in the corner of my heart
        far from
        the eyes of anyone.

Yet, God spied my hidden treasure, and smiling,
        asked if I'd dare bring
        that MORE in me to life,
        new life,
                for all like me
                who dream and ache for more than Law.

I swallowed hard, but
        I
        said
        YES!
I surrendered to birth
        a bigger dream
                than hearts could capture then.

I said YES
        to birthing MYSTERY
        midst the darkness.

My YES blasted walls
        of Law and custom.
It brought talk,
        sniping,
        pointing fingers,
        stones,
                as I walked
                pregnant with MYSTERY,
                        God's dream.

I remember...
        that dark night,
NO'S
slamming in my face,
locked doors,
far from family,

                    my body bursting
            I gave birth
                        to MYSTERY shining
                        on a bed of straw
                        midst blood and tears,
                        beggars' breath,
                        shepherds' sighs.

            Yes, I remember...
                    hot sand,   night chill,
                        running,   foreign lands,
                            fleeing,   strange streets,
                    fugitives,   Herod's cold cruelty.

            But, I do remember warmer days,
                    watching my boy grow.
            I saw myself in him.
                    I wondered who he might become.
                    I loved his fire,
                            his integrity, his joy.
            And as he grew, I saw
                    his YES,
                        His YES to God   and
                                no one else!

            I was afraid.
            Mother love could not last longer.
            He was a young man
                    with the future in his eyes, and
                            compassion in his arms!

            I let him go.
            I let him go into his YES,
                        into streets,
                        salons,
                            and synagogues,
            open arms of prostitutes and beggars,   and
                    into the slippery hands of hypocrites!

            I am a martyr's mother.

            I let him go into his YES.
            I let him go into God's arms.
            GOD'S ARMS BECAME A CROSS!

            And my YES
            hung limp
            on the tree—
                    a last
                    lifeless

leaf.

I cried all martyrs' mothers' tears.
I wailed the death of dreams and hoping.
I moaned my flesh and blood
      martyr-child snatched
      too young
      from the nest!

WHERE ARE YOU NOW GOD?

WHO ARE YOU
      TO LET GO OF
           YOUR PEARL
               SO EASILY?

WHAT KIND OF CRUEL GOD ARE YOU
      THAT SNUFFS OUT
           YOUR OWN DREAM?

HE GAVE YOU EVERYTHING.
YOU GAVE HIM DEATH!

SCORPIONS!

SNAKES!

YOU GAVE US STONES, NOT BREAD!

But, I remember...
      how there was new
           breath
               and wind
                  and blessing.
      how God
           breathed
              into our empty.

Death couldn't hide,
Death couldn't hold our YES!

Yes! there was breath
      and bread
           and blessing!

YES! An empty tomb! YES!
      bread broken and blessed on a road! YES!

ARMS OPENED
      AND HEARTS BURNING WITHIN US! YES!

There is breath
     and wind
       and blessing! YES!

He lives!
among us!

I birthed a bigger dream
     more than our lives,
     more than our hearts
         could contain,
     more truth than
       death's arms could bear!

Dreams lie waiting, hidden
     in your hearts to be born again
        carried to all who long like us for MORE.

My sisters, my brothers,
     carry them, bear them.
Bring them to YES!
Bring them to birth
     midst the darkness!

The Woman with the Flow of Blood

She emerges out of the stories of Mark 5, Matthew 9 and Luke 8.
Her hemorrhage violated the laws of ritual purity; she was alien-
ated, scorned. In the poem, the emphasis on 'unclean' relates to
the laws of ritual impurity and should not be read in an anti-
Jewish way. In her encounter with Jesus and His teaching she
found the courage to claim the integrity which was hers by birth
and which belongs to all who enter God's Reign. After Jesus broke
through the blood taboo to heal her, she becomes an evangelist to
those whose honor has been stolen from them — to all women
who have found shame in their bodies, their menstrual blood,
and to all people who have suffered from the wounds of sexual
and physical violence.

THE WOMAN WITH THE FLOW OF BLOOD

I am God's song
          of tender healing.

My name was TABOO!
          "SHE IS UNCLEAN!"
          "SHE IS STAINED!"

For twelve years
          my affliction was a
                    bloody badge,
          an insult to God's immaculate
                                        inviolable NAME.

For twelve years I sought
          healers, herbs, and promise,
          trying to buy back my possibilities.

My funds spent,
nothing remained
save
     my blood and
          shame.

But a Nazarene
          began to preach among us.
He told stories of a God
          who loved the losers, unmentionables,
                    like me.

One spring morning
I wrapped up
in my ragged
          cloak of shame
and followed him.

The crowd swarmed
          like hornets.
He made his way
          to see a sick girl
          (a rich man's daughter).

As he walked, he talked:
His God was a Mother
          Hen who loved
                    her fragile
                    young.

His God
  sung a poor
    woman's song,
      searching
        for her
        last sheep,
        her lost
          coin,

His God
    loved
    search
        as much
        as sacrifice!

Trailing behind,
I crept along,
  face hidden,
  heart straining
  to catch
        pictures of
          the God
          my blood
          rebuked.

Then someone
      hissed:
        "UNCLEAN!"
Their pointing
        pushed me
            down
        and left me
            lost,
        choking salt
              and dust.

But in the quiet,
        swallowing tears,
        I heard his God crying
        out for what was
        crushed and
        lost and
          left behind
              in me.

His God
    pleading like
    a mother
    for my healing,
    my wholeness,
    for my stolen honor!

I heard
God whispering my name!
Hope
    rose out
    of the
    dust in me
    and wrapped
    round me ——
        a cloak of righteousness!

I sprung up and
like an arrow
      sliced through
      the crowd
      till
      I
      hovered ·
      an arm's length
      at his back.

My blood rushed.
My hand darted—
      adder-tongued —to
      touch the tassel
      of his cloak.

Was it a second? a minute?
I stood.
Time stopped.
The twelve year
      shame
      stopped,
      stanched.

He stopped.
"WHO TOUCHED ME?
WHO CONJURED SO MUCH LIFE FROM ME?"

I   kept quiet
  (someone else
    would surely speak).
Silence weighed
like a stone.

My truth, gagged,
could wait no longer,
      "IT WAS I, TEACHER!"

The serpents hissed, and venom flew,
    "Lord, she is...
        UNCLEAN,
      Surely you know THE STAINED WOMAN......"

Jesus did not hear.

He took my hand,
He pronounced my name:

"HONORED DAUGHTER OF SARA,
YOU HEARD GOD SPEAK
          THROUGH ALL YOUR SHAME.
     YOU RISKED ALL YOU HAD TO HEAR!"

And then my story flowed
          out and over...
          my pain, my search.
I proclaimed the tender heart of God
who loved my blood
          more than burnt offering,
who loved my life as much as LAW!
"Who could imagine
     such a God
          who holds and heals
          untouchables?"

Some stood by and whispered,
          some sucked in their cheeks.
Others walked away.

But Jesus, the Teacher,
     raised his arms and laughed,

"SISTER,
          TODAY
               YOU TELL US GOD'S TRUTH.
     LISTEN, ALL WITH
          EARS TO HEAR!"

"WOMAN, GO
          IN PEACE.
     PROCLAIM YOUR
          MEMORIES.
     GO, TO ALL THE LOST AND LEFT BEHIND.
     YOU ARE GOD'S WITNESS!"

And so,
          from the mountaintops
          and from the valleys
I announce
     a God
     who holds our names
     like treasure,
     who cries out for our stolen hope,
     and who sends us
               as the healing
                    from all shame.
"Listen, all with ears to hear!"

The Bent Over Woman

She is mentioned in Luke 13. She is a broken woman who through
Jesus' healing, claims her power and impatience. She channels
her anger to challenge the deeds of those who continue to keep
others in legal bondage. She becomes a symbol and spokeswoman
for many women today whose gifts for ministry and service are
restricted and denied in church and society.

THE BENT OVER WOMAN

I am God's shout of liberty!
Free from yokes and fetters!

I am your sister.
        I sing my own song now,
            but it was not always so.

For eighteen years
I lived like a twisted limb,
            bent in shame.
I carried sin in heavy sacks.
My yoke: my worthlessness before them all,
My guilt: for what?
            I never knew.

A beast burdened, bent, I bore disgrace
            and could not raise my head
                    to anyone,
                        to hope,   to sky.
I had no face. I had no voice.
I had no need of them.
I was spurned and punished.
(They said by God).

One temple Sabbath
as I hung back
the teacher spied me
        in my hidden spot, and,
            as if I had a face,
he bid me come to him.

I shuffled along,
        seeing only floor,
            but feeling eyes of all,
                like owls at night
                    on my back.
My head bowed low,
I heard the mumbling,
            the rattling
                of those old tongues.

I stood before him, all
        hang-headed, waiting.

He touched me.
He touched my bent and knotted back.
He touched my head,
            my face,

He dared caress what was
        disgrace,
        ugly,
        misshapen!

Bending low, he whispered,
    "FREE!"
And again, "WOMAN, YOU ARE FREE!"

The yoke split!
    Ten thousand fragments s c a t t e r e d !   f l o w n !

And slowly, ever so,
one
by one,
I pulled.

I pulled at
stiff
and
useless
muscles.

With tears,
and sweat streaming,
short breaths stabbing, I labored for my life!

Courage rise in me like lava!

Till I lifted
my bones
up,
stretched
in pain's protest
to my
full height,
trembling, a-quiver like a new born foal!

I faced the crowd.
I faced the teacher.

He looked into my eyes
and smiled
"SISTER,
       YOU WILL NEVER BEAR SHAME AGAIN
       LIKE A BEAST!"

And right there, I stretched back my stiff arms,
I threw back my head, and
I danced my God a song of rightness!
I danced a song of freedom around them all.
(And they began to argue with the teacher about a rule).

Some spoke to me,
          "Woman, stop! You are irreverent!"

          "Why so impatient? Couldn't you have waited one
          more day for healing?"

          "It's the Law!"

Can you imagine,
          wait another day?

They argued still
and I glorified God.

Again the Pharisees
called me impatient.

I stopped my dance.
I spoke.

"YOU ARE RIGHT.
I AM IMPATIENT!
BECAUSE
I
HAVE WAITED LONG ENOUGH
FOR GOD.
BUT TODAY
GOD HEARD THE CRY OF THE MISBEGOTTEN.
GOD HELPED US CLAIM FULL STATURE!"

Today I am Sarah's daughter,
I am Miriam's sister.

I am the mustard tree
          all wide-branched,
                    embracing sky and hope!
I am the pillar of fire
          leading us out of slavery.
I am the gate for all
          who have no face, no future.

I am your sister. I sing the songs
          of freedom for those who have no song yet.

You are right.
I am impatient, yes! But
We have waited long enough.

And we will rejoice
and we will dance
whenever and wherever
we find God's graciousness.

There are no wrong
          days to claim one's birthright.
There are no wrong places
          to find and sing one's song.

Now is the acceptable time.
Every day is sacred.

Mary of Magdala

Mary is a mysterious woman. The Gospels contain little evidence to substantiate the myths and legends about her status as a "reformed prostitute," or about her relationship with Jesus. However, each Gospel does refer to Mary of Magdala's presence at Jesus' crucifixion and burial or to her witness to the empty tomb and the Risen Jesus. In her story I discovered a woman who understood all too well the geography of sorrow and emptiness in her own heart. Her friendship with Jesus helped to heal her painful memories. Her encounter with His Risen Presence contained a commission to gather all the broken-hearted of history and to proclaim to them her story of unbelievable good news.

MARY OF MAGDALA

I sing songs
      from empty tombs.
I sing of dawn's dance
      with darkness.
I am Mary of Magdala.

I met him in my emptiness.
I was my tomb then.
My spirit had died long before.
My body, an empty gourd.
My heart, a hollow hideout
     for any lost,
          wild spirit.
I was my own tomb then,
    and the squatter spirits raged,
            ransacked my   house of bone.

I first met him
     in my emptiness.
He was like no other.
He embraced my wilderness.
He was like no other.
He loved me with gentle fierceness.
His love was no squatter.
He filled the caverns of my hollow heart
    and welcomed me home.

He helped me sift through shards
     of dreams and frozen tears.
He helped me reclaim my treasure.
He danced delight
     at so much God in me,
     too long hidden.
He bid my goodness rise,
     a swollen river,
      flooding the banks of broken promises,
     washing my ragged, wounded spirit.

And I rose from my tomb
     shining, warm,
     and tall in my truth!

But let me sing you another empty tomb.
It was a dark Sabbath's ending,
     no dancing, only dirges.

I wanted just one more time
     with him.
One more time to bathe his battered body

in my thankful tears.
One more time to anoint him
    with my heart's myrrh.
One more time to wrap him in the memories
    of love and dreams
    and dancing in the moonlight
    long after all had gone to sleep.

And on this morning
    all I found
    was emptiness,
        my old wound
            gashed open.

Who would deny me a final farewell?
In the early morning
        moon's light
I wept a raging river.
I mourned stolen memories.
I mourned the death of love.

"MARY",

I heard my name,
The gardener chasing me away....

"Go ahead, take me too,
but I will not leave!
until I make my farewell!
That you can not steal from me!"

"MARY . . ."

"Leave me alone!"

"MARY . . ."

(Wait, this voice was no gardener, no soldier...
This voice was tender.
This voice bid my heart rise and dance!)

He appeared with dawn.
We wept in wonder.
And we danced — we danced —
    (trumpets may have blared)

We danced in the dawn light,
    clothes streaming.
    (choruses may have echoed at the wonder of it)
We sighed surprise and wept diamonds!
We danced.

(midst horns and drums and people cheering
HOSANNAH!   HOSANNAH!)

Then, he stopped.
He spoke,

"MARY DO NOT CLING. GO. GO NOW.
GO, GATHER THEM.
GATHER THE SHARDS OF DISAPPOINTMENT
AND DESPAIR,
THE BROKEN HEARTED.
GATHER THE MEMORIES.
GATHER THE GOODNESS.

"TELL THEM, 'DO NOT BE AFRAID'.
TELL THEM TO FOLLOW YOU.
I GO AHEAD TO GALILEE.
GO NOW."

And so, my heart is full,
my feet carry me, racing to you,
gathering tears and tragedy,
broken hearts like wildflowers.

My sisters, brothers, rise!
Come out of tombs, let life rise in you
like dawn from darkness!

The Canaanite Woman

She appears in Mark 7 and Matthew 15. She is a Gentile. At this point in his journey Jesus does not see himself called to assist Gentiles. However, as an outsider her persistent and stubborn faith, which seems wider than that of Jesus, like that of Jesus' example of the woman before the unjust judge opens Jesus' eyes. She becomes a temporary, unexpected Spiritual Director for Jesus, providing him with new directions and insights. Her tenacity takes her back to her own Gentile people and to all who wait as outcasts on the boundaries of our society, with the invitation to enter a world once closed to them.

THE CANAANITE WOMAN

I am the Canaanite woman.
    I sang out
      our hunger for wholeness
      at the gates of God's banquet!

In our heart's famine
    I risked
    a last pinch
    of faith
    for my daughter,
    for our future.

"Jesus! Son of David!
Israel's child!
Stop! Have pity on me!
    For my child,
    our hope,
    lies longing,
    wasting
      at your gates of plenty!
Hear us begging for life!

"You, Jesus, silent as
    stone,
    standing there,
    filled with
    milk and with honey
    for the children of Israel,
Hear my cause!

"You, Jesus, hiding there,
    locking the doors
      of your feast,
        flowing fat
          with bread
            and baskets of kindness
              left over,
Hear me!

"Hear me!
I won't stop my pounding!
I won't go away!
No one can silence my howling!
    I am a thunderstorm,
    I'll batter your barricades with my shouting,
    I'll wear away stones with my tears!
    I am spring lightning!
    I'll split wide open
      the frozen tongues of time!"

"Break open your borders,
Stretch out your reign's ropes!
Untie your God's arms.

Unbind your God's dreams.
Jesus, set your God free!

"Your God is the one
            Maker of mountains
                        and sky,
            rain and sun
                        washing us all,
            soil and sand
                        receiving our step,
                        giving growth to our seed.
Your God is the one
            Giver of breath and of
                        birth and of dreams!

"How can your God
            who feeds leper
                        and sinner
            spit on the face of the Canaanite children?
If your God is a mother,
            there is room in her arms,
            there is room at her breast
                        for us all!

"Jesus, I believe
            in your God,
            but I don't need seats
            at your banquet.
I know at God's table
            scraps fall
                        as the lost sheep
                                    of Israel
                                                gobble their fill.

"Just throw me   the shreds of
            God's   mercy
            through the gates of your heart.
I can find fullness
            with fragments
                        left over!"

A great silence followed my storm.
Then, a rattle,
            a clank
                        of old chains.
Then music,
            loud laughter.

His heart flaps stretched
    open.
      He ushered me in.

"WOMAN,
    YOUR FAITH
    IS NO SCRAP,
IT'S GOD'S BANQUET!

YOUR DAUGHTER
    IS HEALED.
    RUN, FIND HER,
    FIND FRIENDS,
      ALL WHO ARE FAMISHED.
WE ALL MUST FEAST AT YOUR TABLE OF FAITH!"

So, my sisters, my brothers,
    who hunger for wholeness,
    come, gather!
Feast on the bless'd bread of compassion
    stout wine of justice
    and the generous fullness of God!

Mary of Bethany

She is found in Mark 14, Matthew 26, Luke 10, and John 12. As
Elisabeth Schüssler Fiorenza points out in her book, *In Memory
of Her*, Mary is the true disciple. She is a woman faithful to the
truth of her own being: she was blessed with a strong intellect
and was compelled to break barriers to seek and listen carefully to
the teachings denied women of her day. Her understanding,
coupled with her compassion, enabled her to become a "do-er of
the Word," to minister to Jesus with the care and courage in the
moment of fear and anguish.

MARY OF BETHANY

I am Mary of Bethany.
I sing a disciple's song
        unstopped by sirens
            of terror
            and doors of death!

Housekeeping could not
        keep me
        in my exile from the Torah
            and the Prophets of my people.
I stole manna
        eavesdropping
        through cracks in walls and doors
        gathering basketfuls
        from their learned conversations.
Till one day
Lazarus
brought home
a   Rabbi who caught
        my curiosity
            creeping through the keyhole, uninvited.

But he embraced it, and
            welcomed me in.
Wordless,
I found my place among them.
My home,
now,   a Promised Land.

My mind unlocked,
my tongue unleashed,
        questions stuffed too long inside
           came
             tumbling out
                like seed
                  from bursting sacks.

We squandered hours long
        after sunset, learning.
We stopped when we
        had no more questions,
            no more night to spend.

I knew he had no more
        days to spend with us
        when he dined here
        six days before Passover.

That night
terror
joined those men
around our table.

Thick doors
slammed shut on me,
        and they locked themselves
                into fear's cold clutches.

Left outside,
        no manna came my way,
        only raucous laughter,
        nervous noise
        slipped through slits
        of their bravado.

What a waste of bread
                and wine,
                and friendship!
Trying to outshout
        death's silent sadness!
What a waste of time and words!

Locked doors could not keep
        my disciple's tongue tied.

Breaking through
        fear's waxy seal,
        doors flung wide,
        I burst in!

Silence stung.
        I threw myself
        at the Rabbi's feet.

        "Jesus, you'll soon die!
        Why waste the time
        we have on fear?

        "Why save nard
        for death's day?"

        First his head,
        "It gives no comfort then."

        Then his feet,
        "You are prophet,
        anointed for the painful days ahead."

        I smeared
        the dripping oil all over him.
        I poured out my love

with nard and salt
·weeping wildly all the tears
those men
dared not shed that night.

Heavy stillness,
sweet sorrow, filled the room.

A voice sliced the thickness.

"LORD, SHE IS TOO MUCH...
WASTEFUL...
A BOTHER!
LET US SEND HER AWAY!"

A slow sigh . . .

"JUDAS, JUDAS,
SILVER NEVER SAVES
THE POOR, NOR
WILL IT SAVE YOU!
LEAVE HER ALONE!
LISTEN TO HER.
SHE LISTENED WELL TO ME,
MY WORD
SUNK DEEP
INTO HER HEART
LIKE SEED!
HERE IS ONE DISCIPLE
WITH TRUTH TO HARVEST – one hundred-fold!

"LEAVE HER ALONE!
WHAT SHE HAS DONE
WILL NEVER BE FORGOTTEN.

"WHAT SHE HAS DONE
WE MUST ALSO DO
FOR EACH OTHER.

"LISTEN TO HER.
BREAD AND SILVER
NEVER SAVE.
ONLY LOVE,
LIKE OIL AND TEARS
SPILLED INTO OUR LOCKED HEARTS
BREAKS DOWN OUR FEAR.

"WHAT SHE HAS DONE,
YOU MUST ALSO DO, LONG AFTER
I LEAVE YOU...

LISTEN!"

The Woman at the Well

Found in John 4 and 5, she is an outsider, outcast by her Samaritan background, her questionable lifestyle, and her status as a woman. She seems sullen; she is despairing. In her "showdown at high noon" with Jesus, she discovers the waters of fullness and grace for which she has been thirsting all her life. Like all who discover God's spirit dwelling within them, she finds a new voice and a new vocation: she becomes a most unlikely, yet very convincing first messenger of the God within to her own Samaritan people.

THE WOMAN AT THE WELL

I am a Samaritan woman.
I was born
with a dust storm
twisting
in my soul.

As I grew I had no child's
          song,
only cries,
          while thirst's ember
                    smoldered in my scorched soul.

My roots shallow,
I roamed from hope
          to dream,
          and sucked short sweetness
          from promises
          that dried like dust
                    on my lips.

From teachers
I begged rain
          for my tender roots.
Their scorn
          choked like
          sand
          in my throat.

I rushed to drink my fill
          of God's truth,
but rabbis guarded gates saying
          I was unclean,
          I couldn't enter
          lest I sour the rivers of God.

I bathed in the passion
          and the favors of men.
But all was delusion
          rising like vapor
          in the heat of my longing.

My sole sister,
          noonday sun,
          walked with me.
          My hope withered.
          My heart grew hard.
My mouth stocked stones
          for those whose stares
                    were sticks,
                    poking,

tearing
my thin wall of being.

One noon
when others were inside,
I stood at the well.

A Jew without a jar
        asked me for a drink.
I sized him up.

"Give you a drink?
Leave me alone!
Don't you know
        my thirst draws ash?
        my jar spills
                spoiled water?
Stay away!"

He stood his ground.
He would not leave.
He shook his head.

He said
there was another well
        closer, deeper
        where water
        lived forever
        beneath the sands
                of longing.

"Give me THIS water, sir!
Show me the path!
Take me!
Take my jar!"

He smiled,
asked me to follow.
I took him in.

We descended
    breaking
    layers of lies,
            lovers,
                and loss —

Till his words tapped
        my bedrock,
        snapping and
        cracking it open!

Life ripped wide open within me
      spewing showers of dreams
            and hopes long forgotten!

I gulped at
      the God gushing in me
          leaping like geysers
            rolling, splashing my soul.

I played!
     I danced
          in the pools of my goodness!

Joy roared like a river
      rolling and crashing
      over my banks.
No jar could contain me!

I rushed into town like a flash flood!

"COME AND SEE
      COME AND SEE
      A PROPHET
          WHO ENTERED MY WASTELAND,
          SANG ME MY STORY
          AND STRUCK SPRINGS OF TRUTH
          DEEP IN ME AS
          FROM STONES
             IN THE SINAI!

"WANDER NO FURTHER
      IN YOUR DESERTS
          OF LONGING.

THIS IS OUR CHRIST.
LET HIM LEAD US
      TO WELLSPRINGS OF LIFE!

COME, LET US DRINK DEEPLY
      ALL THE DAYS
         OF OUR LIVES!"

ENDNOTE

This book of poetry by Patricia Clemens Repikoff is published with love by friends of Patty, who believe that the best gift we are able to give her as she leaves St. Thérèse Parish is to return to her this beautiful affirmation of her own informed spirituality, sung in her own words and interpreted visually by others who know her.

Patty Repikoff has been Pastoral Life Director of St. Therese Parish for the past eight years. As a woman in ministry, she is a forerunner. She is a courageous leader of a Catholic Christian faith community. Grounded in her own amazing spirituality, Patty has been present to this community as enabler, fellow traveler in joy and grief, counselor, gifted homilist, astute leader, teacher, friend, happy warrior — and poet.

The Patty we know could write as Mary of Nazareth: Dreams lie waiting, hidden in your hearts, to be born again, carried to all who long like us for more. My sisters, my brothers, carry them, bear them. Bring them to YES! Bring them to birth midst the darkness.

The Patty we know walks in truth and proclaims it memorably. We know her as a woman who brings all the gifts of her sisters as well as her brothers to her ministry. As a forerunner, she can say with her Bent Over Woman: I am your sister, I sing my own song now, but it was not always so.

As we say goodbye this spring to our friend Patty as our parish leader, we know our friendship will continue to be an important part of our continued journey. This little book is to say thank you, God speed, we will remember you.

Woman, go in peace.
Proclaim your memories.

> Members of St. Therese Parish
> Seattle, Washington
> Spring 1998

About the Artists:

Michael Edwards (Mary of Nazareth) a 1996 graduate of St. Therese School, is a sophomore at Seattle Prep and studies at Institute of Realist Art. Her work is presently being shown at Wismer Center for Women, Seattle University. Michael plans to earn a Master of Fine Arts Degree.

Debra Thompson Harvey (The Woman with the Flow of Blood) is a self-taught artist who earned her BA in architecture at the University of Washington. Art, she says, has become her search for depth and soul through creative expression. She works in acrylic on paper, and experiments with monotypes.

Philip Knowles (The Bent Over Woman) a graduate of Otis/Parsons Art Institute in Los Angeles, is trained in the fine arts. He does traditional work including painting and woodblocks, and works as a computer artist for a video game developer.

Cathy Stegman (Mary of Magdala) likes to work in watercolor and ink on watercolor paper. A member of the Shades of Praise Choir, she has a degree in Anthropology and Women's Studies from the University of Washington, and works as a teen parent counselor.

Felicia Hines (The Canaanite Woman) who has attended St. Therese Parish for 12 years, has a degree in art from Seton Hill College. She works in oils, stained glass, clay and pastels "on the side" while she runs a preschool and daycare center.

Hannah Stephens (Mary of Bethany) attends St. Therese with her family, and will be 11 years old in June. She is a fourth grader at Hawthorne Elementary School, and has had a picture published in the Woodland Park Zoo Newsletter. She likes to draw horses, preferring to work in pencil.

Andrea Brganza (The Woman at the Well) has a B.A. in art from The Evergreen College, and works in traditional painting, print making and jewelry. She has coordinated and taught St. Therese School's Fine Arts program. She attended St. Therese School as a child before moving to St. Mary's Parish.